Impressum
Verlag: BABADADA GmbH, Nedderfeld 112 , 22529 Hamburg
Geschäftsführer / Verlagsleitung: Harald Hof
Druck: Books on Demand GmbH, In de Tarpen 42, 22848 Norderstedt

Imprint
Publisher: BABADADA GmbH, Nedderfeld 112 , 22529 Hamburg, Germany
Managing Director / Publishing direction: Harald Hof
Print: Books on Demand GmbH, In de Tarpen 42, 22848 Norderstedt

school

colegio

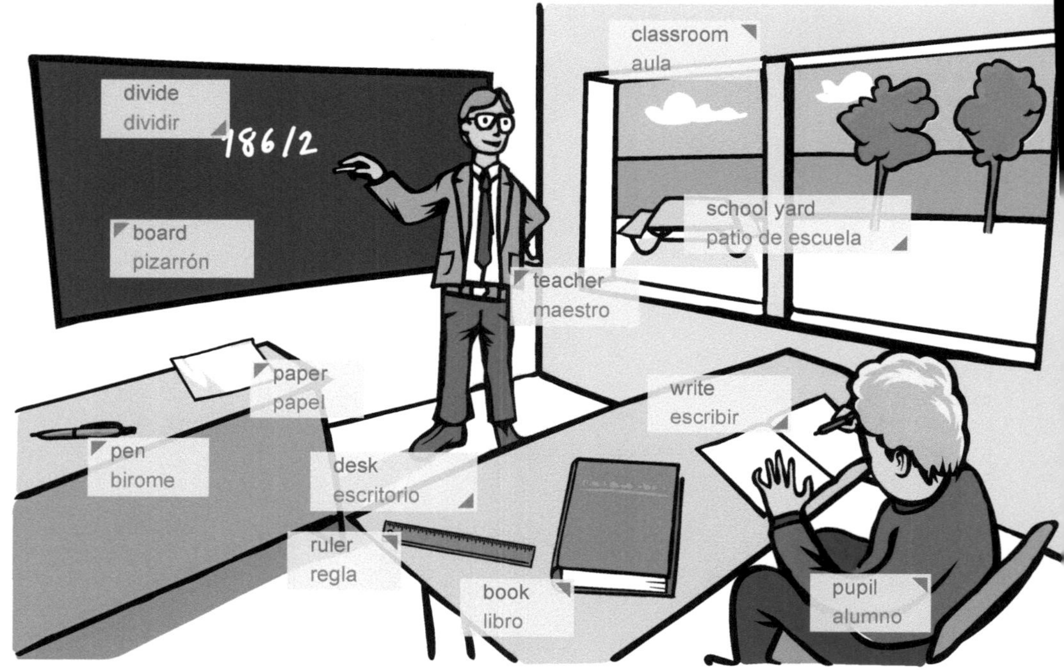
classroom
aula
divide
dividir
186/2
board
pizarrón
school yard
patio de escuela
teacher
maestro
paper
papel
write
escribir
pen
birome
desk
escritorio
ruler
regla
book
libro
pupil
alumno

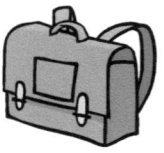

satchel

mochila

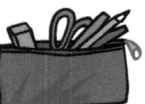

pencil case

caja de lápices

pencil

lápiz

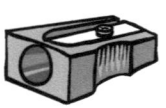

pencil sharpener

sacapuntas

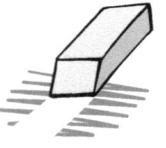

rubber

goma (de borrar)

drawing pad

bloc de dibujo

drawing

dibujo

paintbrush

pincel

paint box

caja de pinturas

scissors

tijera

glue

pegamento

exercise book

cuaderno de ejercicios

homework

tarea

number

número

add

sumar

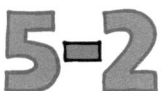

subtract

restar

multiply

multiplicar

calculate

calcular

letter

letra

alphabet

abecedario

word

palabra

text

texto

read

leer

chalk

tiza

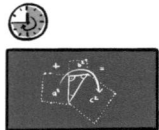

lesson

lección

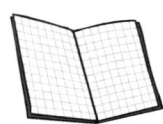

register

cuaderno de clase

exam

examen

certificate

certificado

school uniform

uniforme escolar

education

educación

encyclopedia

enciclopedia

university

universidad

microscope

microscopio

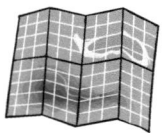

map

mapa

waste-paper basket

tacho (de basura)

hotel
hotel

hostel
hostel

ROOMS

bureau de change
casa de cambio

EXCHANGE

car
auto

language
idioma

yes / no
sí / no

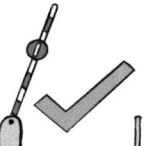

Okay
Está bien

hello
hola

translator
traductor

Thank you
Gracias

how much is...?

¿cuánto cuesta...?

I do not understand

No entiendo

problem

problema

Good evening!

¡Buenas tardes!

Good morning!

¡Buenos días!

Good night!

¡Buenas noches!

bye bye

adiós

direction

dirección

luggage

equipaje

bag

bolso

backpack

mochila

guest

invitado

room

habitación

sleeping bag

bolsa de dormir

tent

carpa

tourist information

información turística

beach

playa

credit card

tarjeta de crédito

breakfast

desayuno

lunch

almuerzo

dinner

cena

ticket

pasaje

lift

ascensor

stamp

sello

border

frontera

customs

aduana

embassy

embajada

visa

visa

passport

pasaporte

transport
transporte

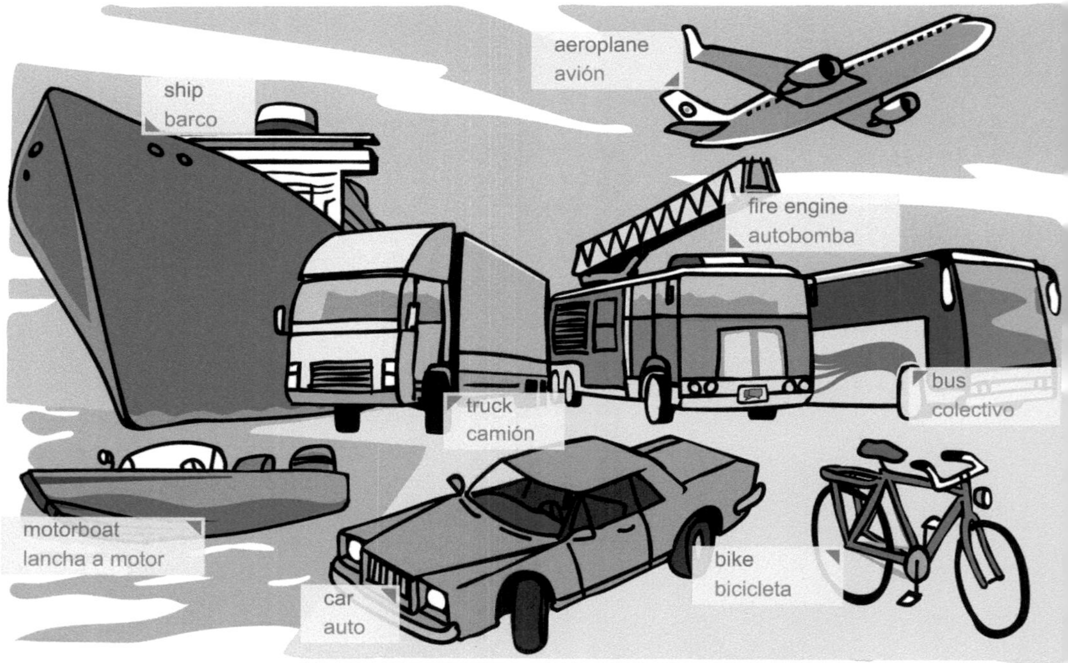
aeroplane
avión
ship
barco
fire engine
autobomba
bus
colectivo
truck
camión
motorboat
lancha a motor
bike
bicicleta
car
auto

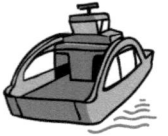

ferry
ferry

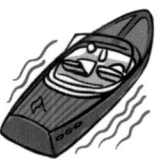

boat
bote

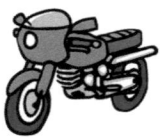

motorbike
moto

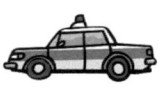

police car
patrullero

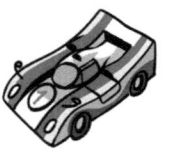

racing car
auto de carreras

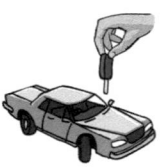

rental car
auto de alquiler

car sharing

alquiler de autos

breakdown truck

grúa

refuse truck

camión de basura

motor

motor

fuel

nafta

petrol station

estación de servicio

traffic sign

señal de tránsito

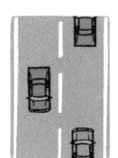

traffic

tránsito

traffic jam

embotellamiento

car park

estacionamiento

train station

estación de tren

tracks

vías

train

tren

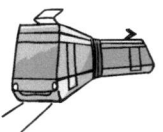

tram

tranvía

carriage

vagón

helicopter

helicóptero

airport

aeropuerto

tower

torre

passenger

pasajero

container

contenedor

carton

caja de cartón

cart

carretilla

basket

canasta

take off / land

despegar / aterrizar

city

ciudad

village

pueblo

city centre

centro de ciudad

house

casa

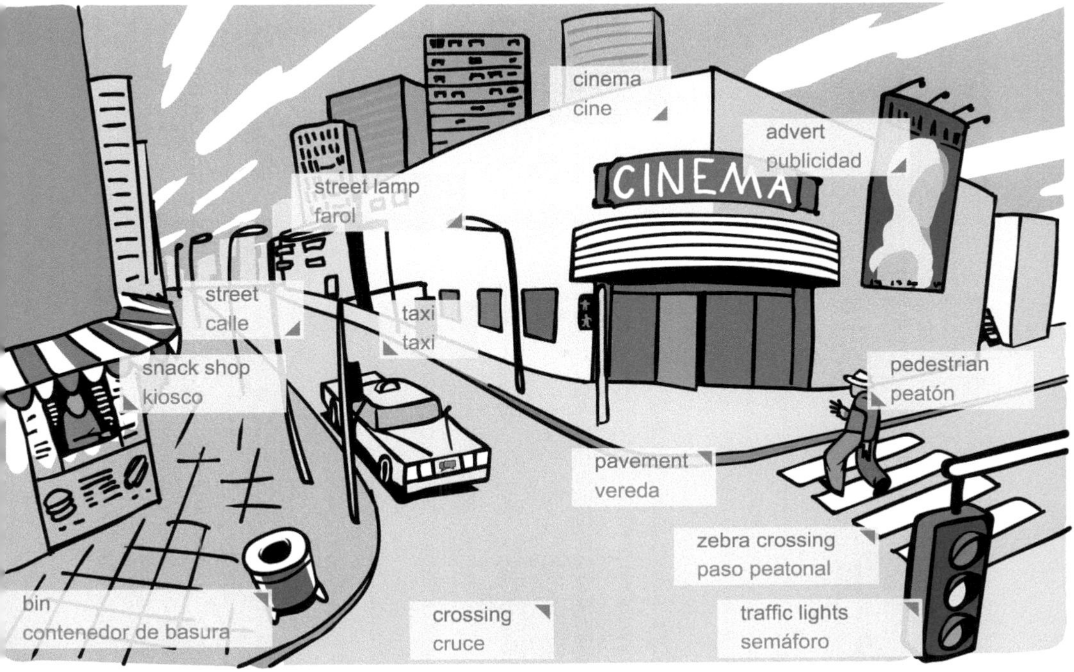

cinema
cine

advert
publicidad

street lamp
farol

CINEMA

street
calle

taxi
taxi

snack shop
kiosco

pedestrian
peatón

pavement
vereda

zebra crossing
paso peatonal

bin
contenedor de basura

crossing
cruce

traffic lights
semáforo

hut
cabaña

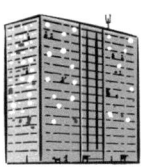

flat
departamento

train station
estación de tren

town hall
municipalidad

museum
museo

school
colegio

university

universidad

bank

banco

hospital

hospital

hotel

hotel

pharmacy

farmacia

office

oficina

book shop

librería

shop

negocio

florist's

florería

supermarket

supermercado

market

mercado

department store

grandes tiendas

fishmonger's

pescadería

shopping centre

centro comercial

harbour

puerto

park

parque

bench

banco

bridge

puente

stairs

escaleras

underground

subte

tunnel

túnel

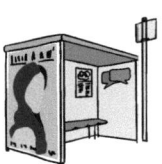

bus stop

parada del colectivo

bar

bar

restaurant

restaurante

postbox

buzón

street sign

letrero

parking meter

parquímetro

zoo

zoológico

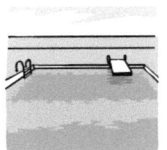

swimming pool

pileta

mosque

mezquita

farm
granja

pollution
contaminación

graveyard
cementerio

church
iglesia

playground
juegos infantiles

temple
templo

landscape
paisaje

signpost
poste indicador

way
camino

meadow
pradera

stone
piedra

tree
árbol

hiker
excursionista

river
río

grass
hierba

flower
flor

valley

valle

hill

montaña

lake

lago

forest

bosque

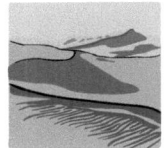

desert

desierto

volcano

volcán

castle

castillo

rainbow

arco iris

mushroom

champiñón

palm tree

palmera

mosquito

mosquito

fly

mosca

ant

hormiga

bee

abeja

spider

araña

landscape - paisaje

beetle

escarabajo

frog

rana

squirrel

ardilla

hedgehog

erizo

hare

liebre

owl

lechuza

bird

pájaro

swan

cisne

boar

jabalí

deer

ciervo

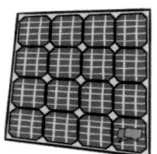

moose

alce

dam

presa

wind turbine

aerogenerador

solar panel

panel solar

climate

clima

restaurant
restaurante

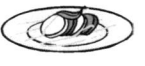

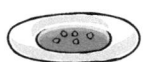

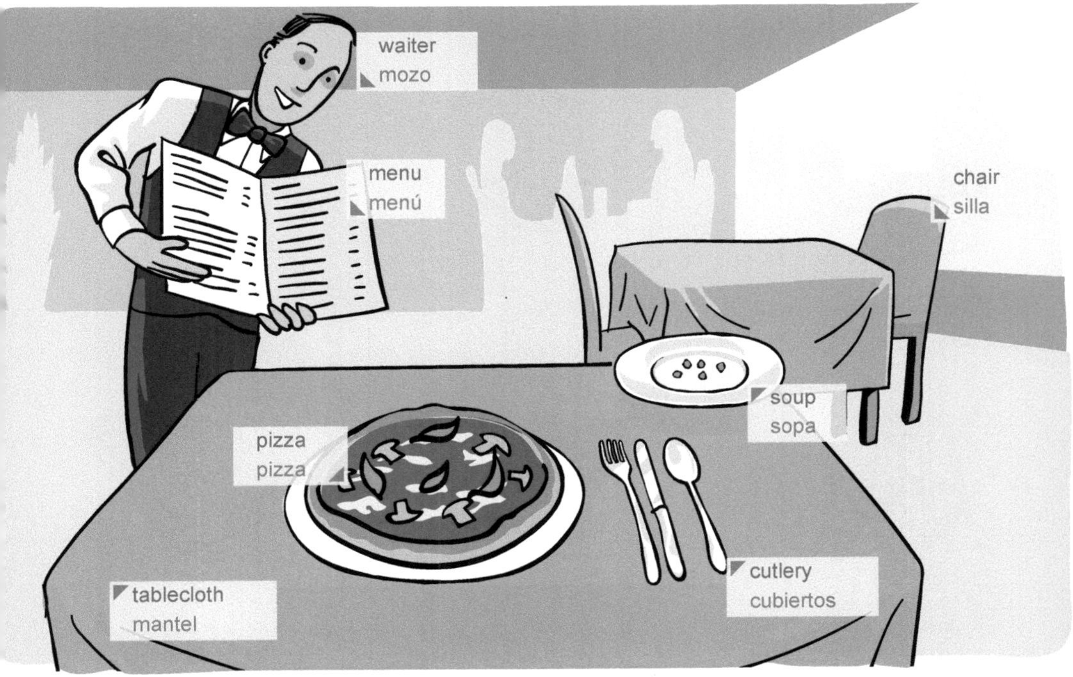
waiter
mozo
menu
menú
chair
silla
soup
sopa
pizza
pizza
cutlery
cubiertos
tablecloth
mantel

starter

entrada

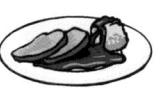

main course

plato principal

dessert

postre

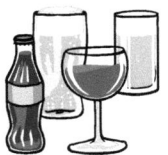

drinks

bebidas

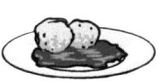

food

comida

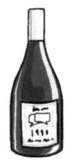

bottle

botella

fast food

comida rápida

street food

comida callejera

teapot

tetera

sugar bowl

azucarera

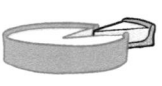

portion

porción

espresso machine

cafetera expreso

high chair

sillita alta

bill

cuenta

tray

bandeja

knife

cuchillo

fork

tenedor

spoon

cuchara

teaspoon

cucharita

serviette

servilleta

glass

vaso

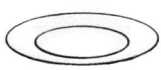

plate

plato

soup plate

plato hondo

saucer

plato

sauce

salsa

salt pot

salero

pepper mill

molinillo de pimienta

vinegar

vinagre

oil

aceite

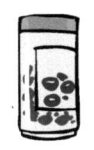

spices

especias

ketchup

kétchup

mustard

mostaza

mayonnaise

mayonesa

supermarket
supermercado

special offer
oferta especial
FOR
customer
cliente
dairy
lácteos
fruit
fruta
trolley
changuito

BUTCHERS

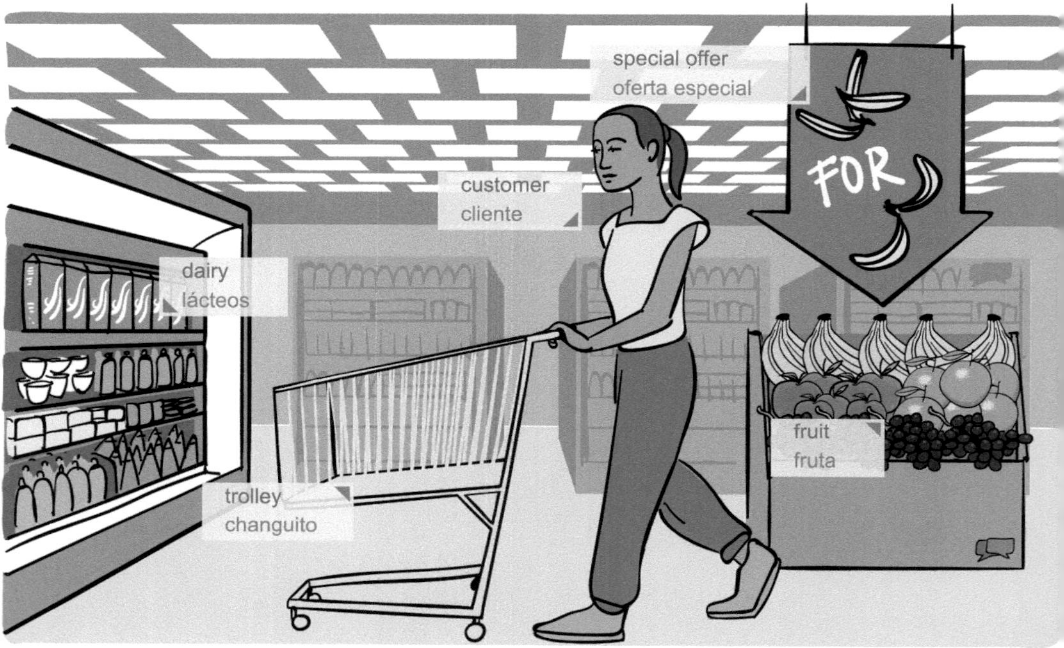

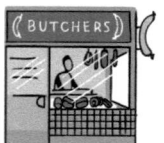

butcher´s

carnicería

BAKERY

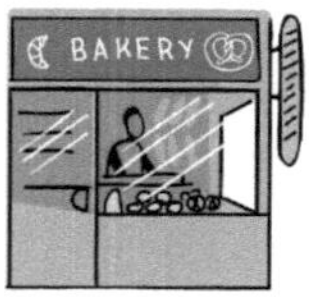

baker´s

panadería

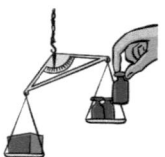

weigh

pesar

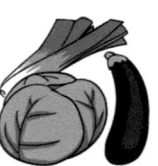

vegetables

verduras

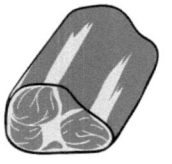

meat

carne

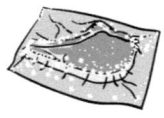

frozen food

alimentos congelados

cold meat
fiambres

tinned food
alimentos enlatados

washing powder
detergente en polvo

sweets
golosinas

household products
electrodomésticos

cleaning products
productos de limpieza

salesperson
vendedora

till
caja

cashier
cajero

shopping list
lista de compras

opening hours
horario de atención

wallet
billetera

credit card
tarjeta de crédito

bag
cartera

plastic bag
bolsa de plástico

supermarket - supermercado

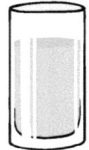

water

agua

juice

jugo

milk

leche

coke

bebida cola

wine

vino

beer

cerveza

alcohol

alcohol

cocoa

cacao

tea

té

coffee

café

espresso

café expreso

cappuccino

cappuccino

banana

banana

apple

manzana

orange

naranja

melon

melón

lemon

limón

carrot

zanahoria

garlic

ajo

bamboo

bambú

onion

cebolla

mushroom

champiñón

nuts

nueces

noodles

fideos

spaghetti

tallarines

rice

arroz

salad

ensalada

chips

papas fritas

fried potatoes

papas fritas

pizza

pizza

hamburger

hamburguesa

sandwich

sándwich

cutlet

churrasco

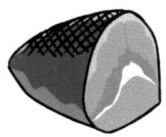

ham

jamón

salami

salame

sausage

salchicha

chicken

pollo

roast

asado

fish

pescado

porridge oats

copos de avena

flour

harina

bread

pan

butter

manteca

egg

huevo

muesli

muesli

croissant

medialuna

toast

tostada

curd

cuajada

fried egg

huevo frito

cornflakes

copos de maíz

bread roll

pancito

biscuits

galletitas

cake

torta

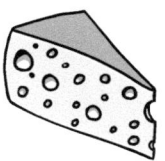

cheese

queso

ice cream

helado

sugar

azúcar

honey

miel

jam

mermelada

chocolate spread

pasta de chocolate

curry

curry

farm
granja

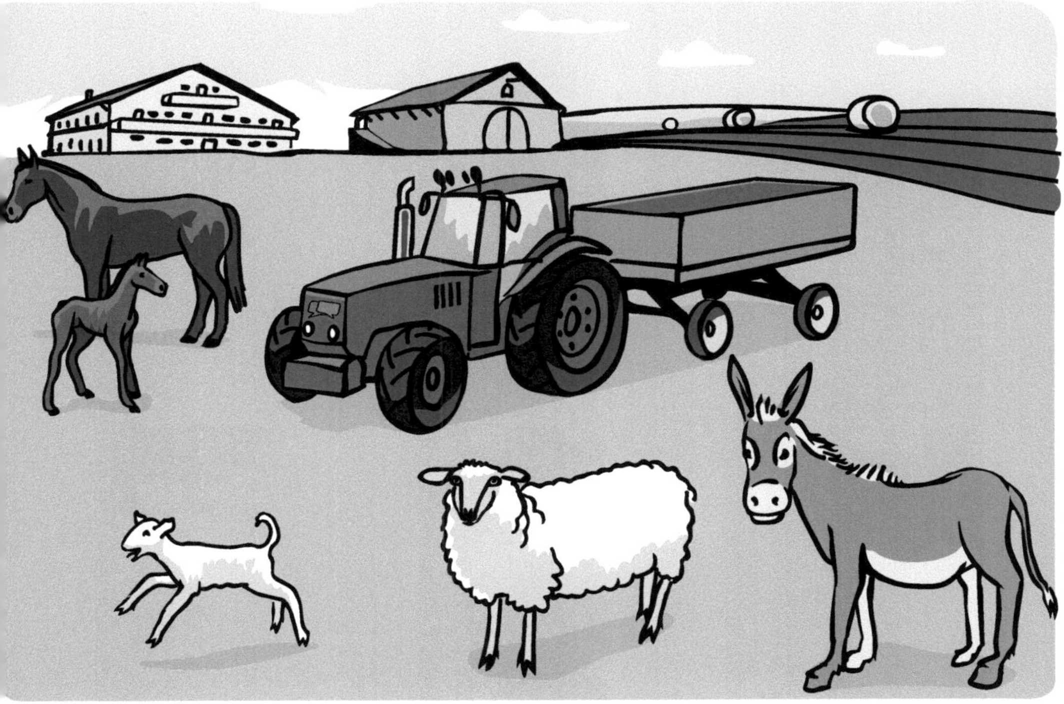

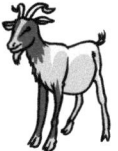

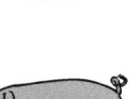

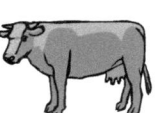

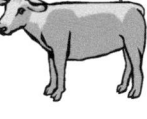

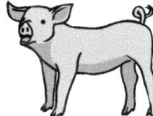

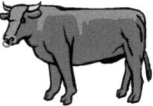

goat

cabra

cow

vaca

calf

ternero

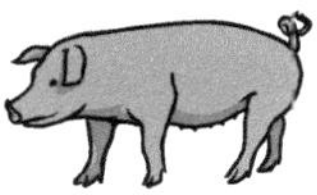

pig

cerdo

piglet

lechón

bull

toro

goose

ganso

duck

pato

chick

pollo

hen

gallina

cock

gallo

rat

rata

cat

gato

mouse

ratón

ox

buey

dog

perro

doghouse

cucha

garden hose

manguera

watering can

regadera

scythe

guadaña

plough

arado

sickle

hoz

hoe

azada

pitchfork

horquilla

axe

hacha

wheelbarrow

carretilla

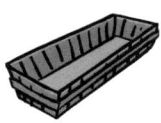

trough

abrevadero

milk can

lechera

sack

bolsa

fence

reja

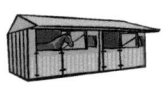

stable

establo

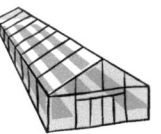

greenhouse

invernadero

soil

suelo

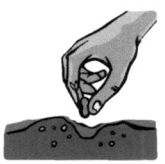

seed

semilla

fertilizer

fertilizador

combine harvester

cosechadora

harvest

cosechar

harvest

cosecha

yams

batatas

wheat

trigo

soy

soja

potato

papa

corn

maíz

rapeseed

semilla de colza

fruit tree

árbol frutal

cassava

mandioca

cereals

cereales

living room
living

bathroom
baño

kitchen
cocina

bedroom
dormitorio

child's room
cuarto de los chicos

dining room
comedor

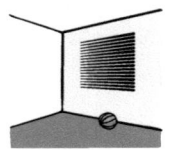

floor

piso

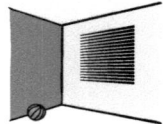

wall

pared

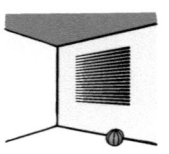

ceiling

cielorraso

cellar

sótano

sauna

sauna

balcony

balcón

terrace

terraza

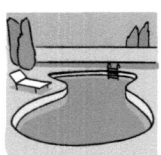

pool

pileta

lawn mower

cortadora de pasto

sheet

sábana

bedspread

acolchado

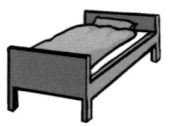

bed

cama

broom

escoba

bucket

balde

switch

interruptor

carpet

alfombra

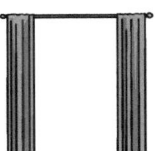

curtain

cortina

table

mesa

chair

silla

rocking chair

mecedora

armchair

sillón

book

libro

blanket

frazada

decoration

decoración

firewood

leña

film

película

hi-fi equipment

equipo de música

key

llave

newspaper

diario

painting

pintura

poster

póster

radio

radio

notepad

cuaderno

hoover

aspiradora

cactus

cactus

candle

vela

kitchen
cocina

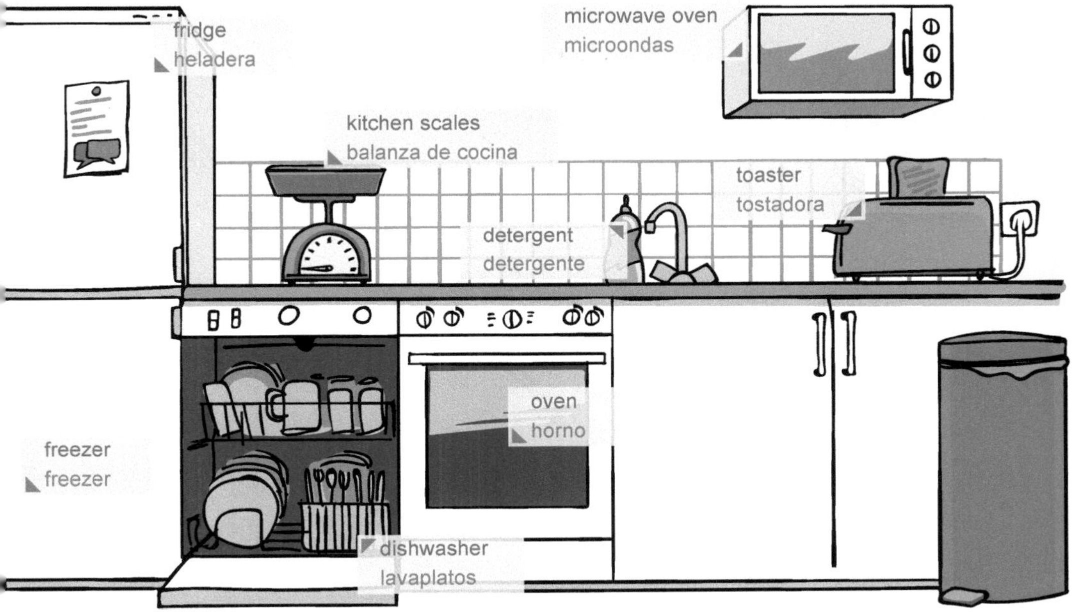
fridge
heladera
microwave oven
microondas
kitchen scales
balanza de cocina
toaster
tostadora
detergent
detergente
oven
horno
freezer
freezer
dishwasher
lavaplatos

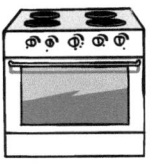

cooker

cocina

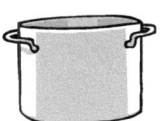

pot

olla

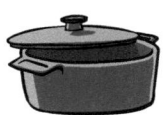

cast-iron pot

olla de hierro fundido

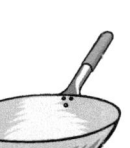

wok / kadai

wok

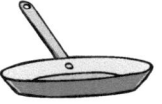

pan

sartén

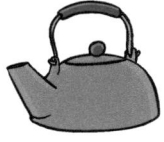

kettle

pava

steamer

vaporera

baking tray

bandeja de horno

crockery

vajilla

mug

taza

bowl

bol

chopsticks

palitos

ladle

cucharón

spatula

estpátula

whisk

batidora

strainer

colador

sieve

colador

grater

rallador

mortar

mortero

barbecue

parrilla

open fire

fogata

chopping board

tabla de picar

rolling pin

palo de amasar

corkscrew

sacacorchos

can

lata

can opener

abrelatas

pot holder

manopla

sink

pileta

brush

cepillo

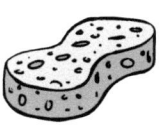

sponge

esponja

blender

batidora

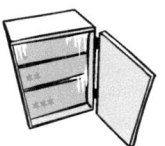

deep freezer

congelador

baby bottle

mamadera

tap

canilla

kitchen - cocina

bathroom

baño

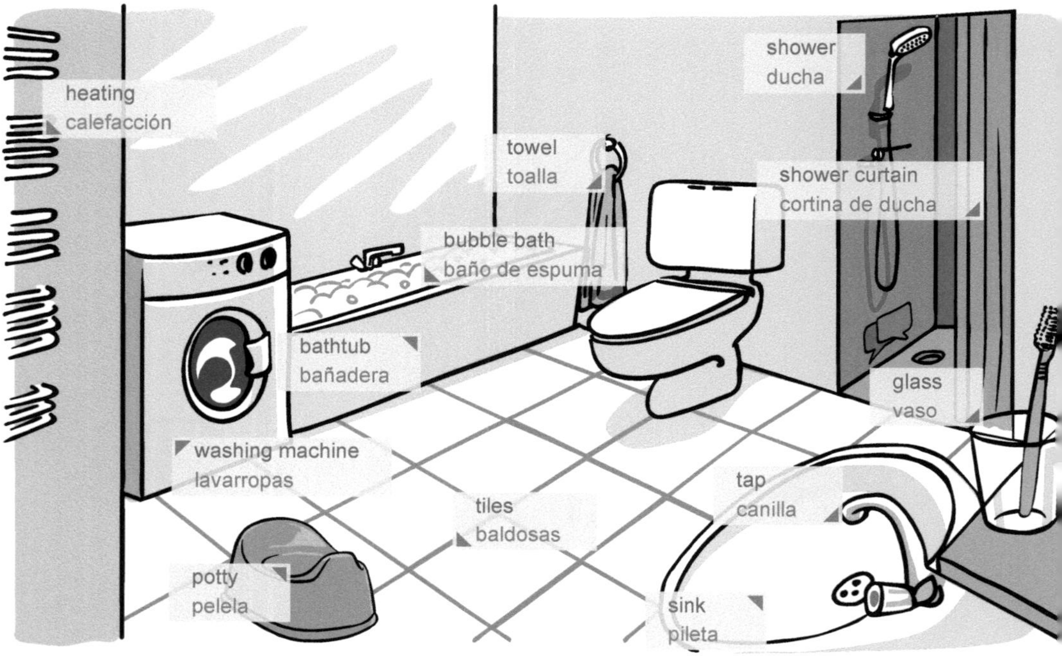

heating
calefacción
towel
toalla
shower
ducha
shower curtain
cortina de ducha
bubble bath
baño de espuma
bathtub
bañadera
glass
vaso
washing machine
lavarropas
tap
canilla
tiles
baldosas
potty
pelela
sink
pileta

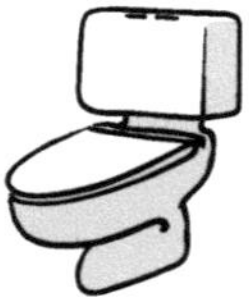

toilet
inodoro

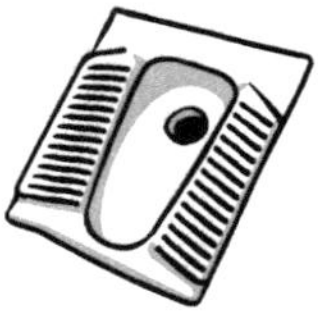

squat toilet
letrina

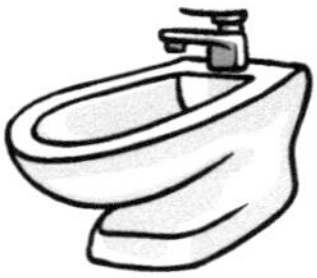

bidet
bidé

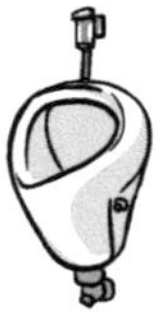

urinal
mingitorio

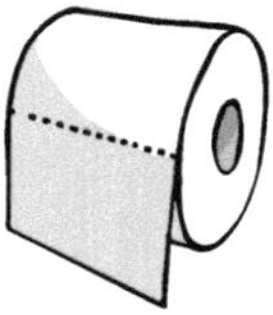

toilet paper
papel higiénico

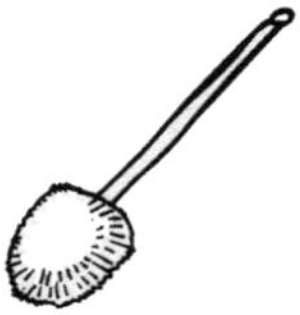

toilet brush
cepillo para el inodoro

toothbrush

cepillo de dientes

toothpaste

dentífrico

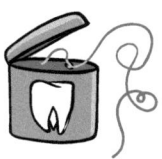

dental floss

hilo dental

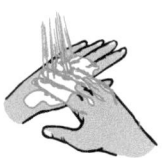

wash

lavar

handheld shower

ducha de mano

douche

ducha higiénica

basin

palangana

back brush

cepillo para espalda

soap

jabón

shower gel

gel de ducha

shampoo

shampoo

flannel

toallita

drain

desagüe

cream

crema

deodorant

desodorante

mirror

espejo

hand mirror

espejito

razor

maquinita de afeitar

shaving foam

espuma de afeitar

aftershave

aftershave

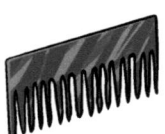

comb

peine

brush

cepillo

hair dryer

secador de pelo

hairspray

spray

makeup

maquillaje

lipstick

lápiz de labios

nail varnish

esmalte para uñas

cotton wool

algodón

nail scissors

tijera para uñas

perfume

perfume

washbag

portacosméticos

stool

banqueta

weighing scale

balanza

bathrobe

bata

rubber gloves

guantes de goma

tampon

tampón

sanitary towel

toallita femenina

chemical toilet

baño químico

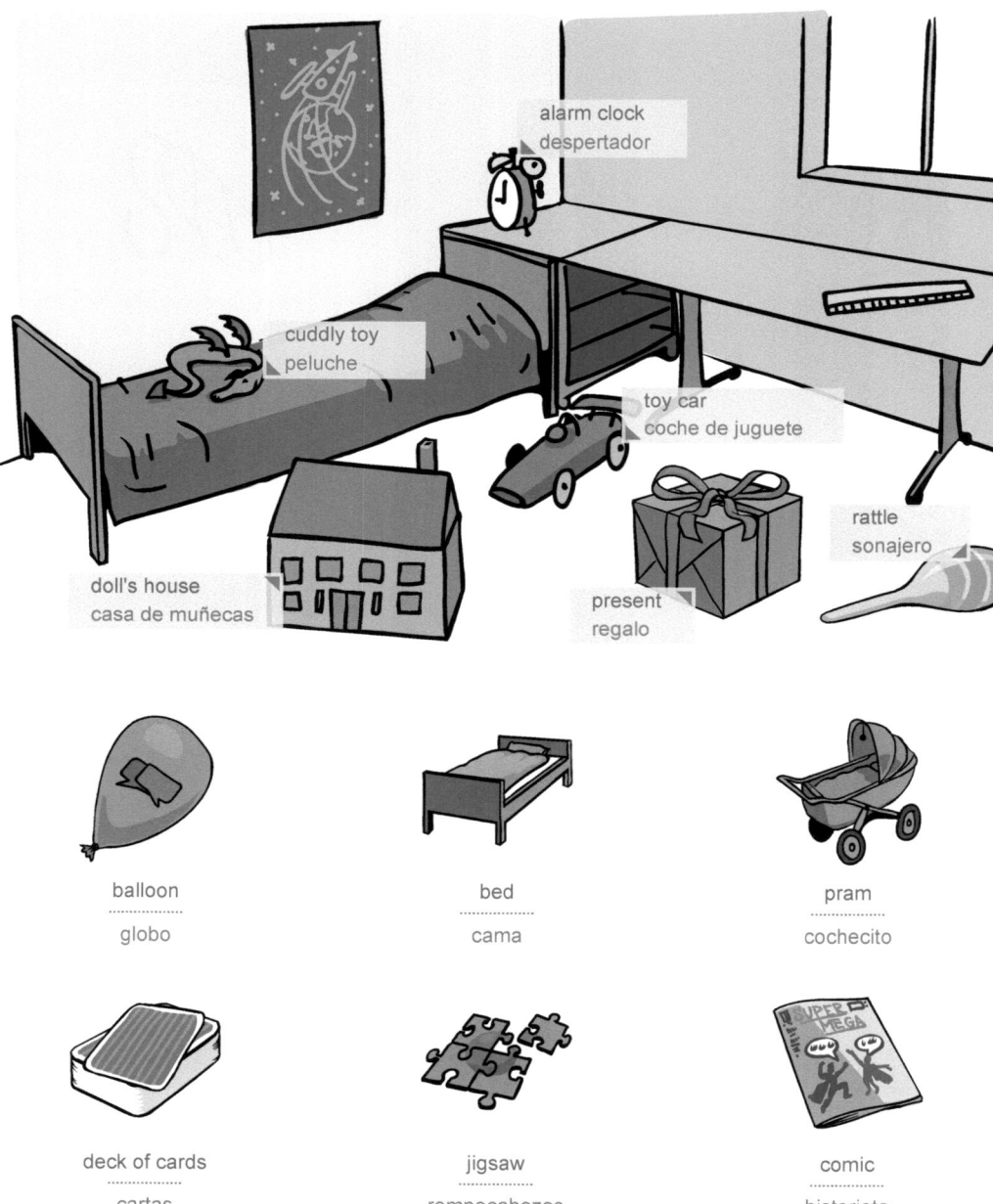

alarm clock
despertador

cuddly toy
peluche

toy car
coche de juguete

rattle
sonajero

doll's house
casa de muñecas

present
regalo

balloon
globo

bed
cama

pram
cochecito

deck of cards
cartas

jigsaw
rompecabezas

comic
historieta

lego bricks

piezas de lego

building blocks

ladrillos de juguete

action figure

figura de acción

babygrow

enterito (de bebé)

frisbee

frisbee

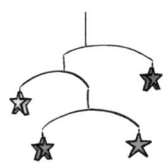

mobile

móvil para bebés

board game

juego de mesa

dice

dados

model train set

tren eléctrico

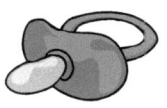

dummy

chupete

party

fiesta

picture book

libro de cuentos ilustrado

ball

pelota

doll

muñeca

play

jugar

child's room - cuarto de los chicos

sandpit

arenero

swing

hamaca

toys

juguetes

video game console

consola de videojuegos

tricycle

triciclo

teddy bear

osito de peluche

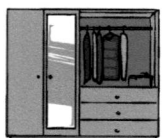

wardrobe

armario

clothing

ropa

socks

medias

stockings

medias panty

tights

calzas

scarf
bufanda

belt
cinturón

umbrella
paraguas

t-shirt
remera

trainers
zapatillas

boots
botas

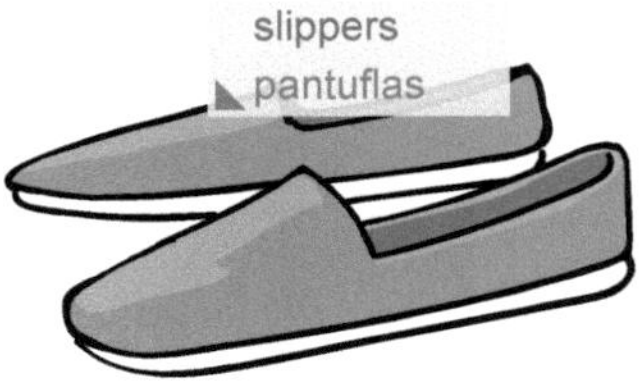

slippers
pantuflas

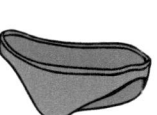

sandals

sandalias

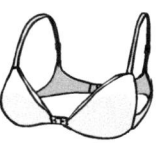

shoes

zapatos

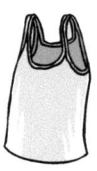

rubber boots

botas de goma

underpants

ropa interior

bra

corpiño

vest

chaleco

body

body

trousers

pantalones

jeans

jeans

skirt

pollera

blouse

blusa

shirt

camisa

pullover

pulóver

hoodie

buzo

blazer

blazer

jacket

campera

coat

tapado

raincoat

piloto

costume

traje

dress

vestido

wedding dress

vestido de novia

suit

traje

nightgown

camisón

pyjamas

pijama

sari

sari

headscarf

pañuelo para cabeza

turban

turbante

burqa

burka

kaftan

caftán

abaya

abaya

swimsuit

traje de baño

trunks

short de baño

shorts

shorts

tracksuit

jogging

apron

delantal

gloves

guantes

button

botón

glasses

anteojos

bracelet

pulsera

necklace

collar

ring

anillo

earring

aro

cap

gorra

coat hanger

percha

hat

sombrero

tie

corbata

zip

cierre

helmet

casco

braces

tiradores

school uniform

uniforme escolar

uniform

uniforme

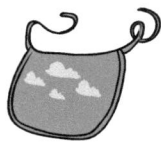

bib

babero

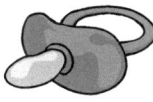

dummy

chupete

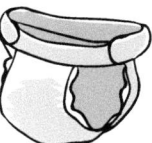

nappy

pañal

office
oficina

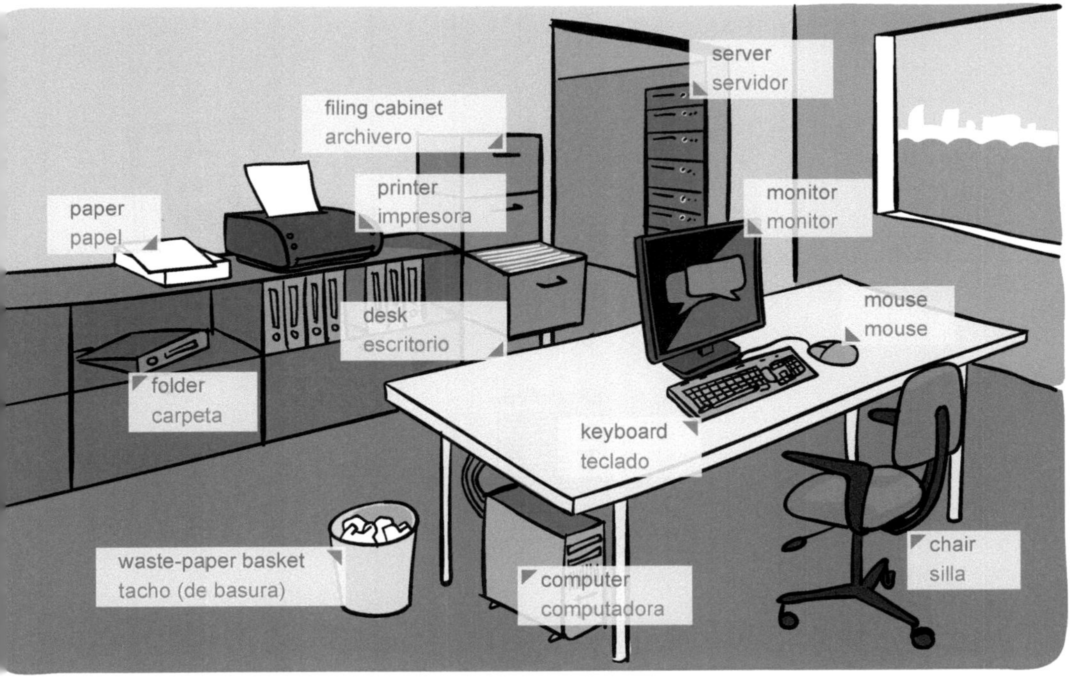
server
servidor
filing cabinet
archivero
printer
impresora
paper
papel
monitor
monitor
mouse
mouse
desk
escritorio
folder
carpeta
keyboard
teclado
waste-paper basket
tacho (de basura)
computer
computadora
chair
silla

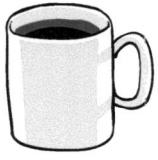

coffee mug

taza de café

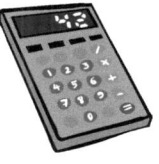

calculator

calculadora

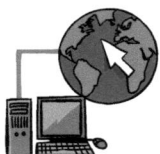

internet

internet

laptop

laptop

letter

carta

message

mensaje

mobile

celular

network

red

photocopier

fotocopiadora

software

software

telephone

teléfono

plug socket

tomacorriente

fax machine

fax

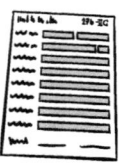

form

formulario

document

documento

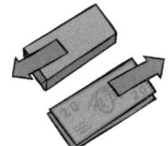

buy

comprar

pay

pagar

trade

hacer negocios

money

dinero

dollar

dólar

euro

euro

yen

yen

rouble

rublo

Swiss franc

franco suizo

renminbi yuan

yuan

rupee

rupia

cashpoint

cajero automático

bureau de change

casa de cambio

gold

oro

silver

plata

oil

petróleo

energy

energía

price

precio

contract

contrato

tax

impuesto

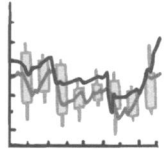

stock

acción

work

trabajar

employee

empleado

employer

empleador

factory

fábrica

shop

negocio

occupations
ocupaciones

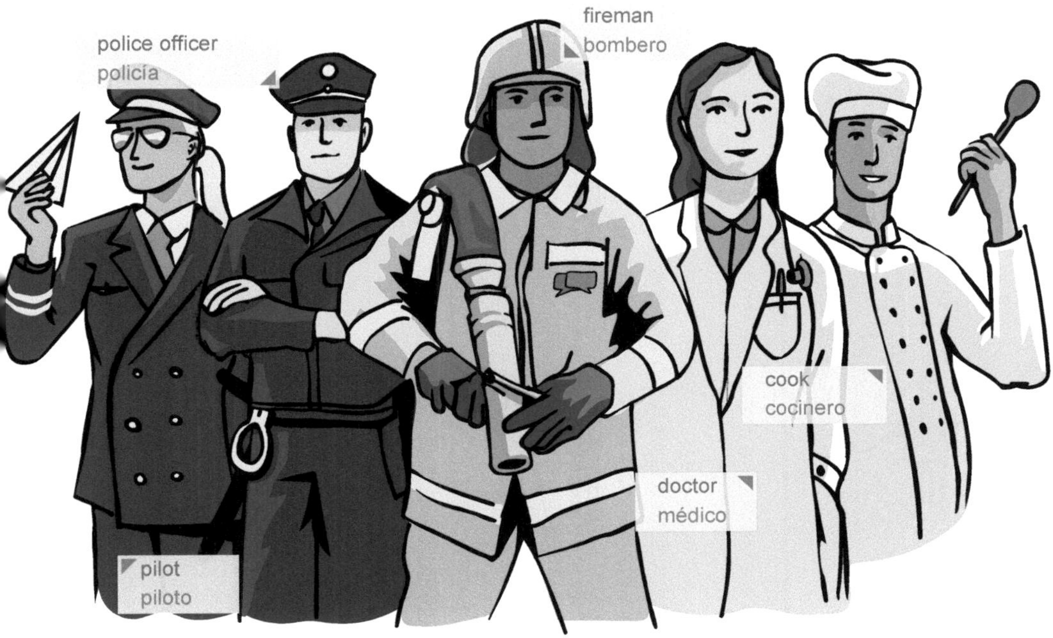

police officer
policía
fireman
bombero
cook
cocinero
doctor
médico
pilot
piloto

gardener

jardinero

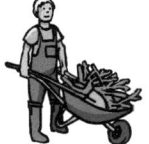

carpenter

carpintero

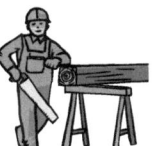

seamstress

modista

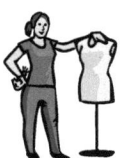

judge

juez

chemist

farmacéutico

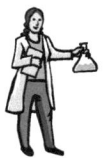

actor

actor

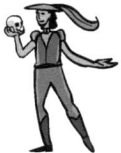

bus driver

colectivero

taxi driver

taxista

fisherman

pescador

cleaning lady

mucama

roofer

techista

waiter

mozo

hunter

cazador

painter

pintor

baker

panadero

electrician

electricista

builder

albañil

engineer

ingeniero

butcher

carnicero

plumber

plomero

postman

cartero

soldier

soldado

architect

arquitecto

cashier

cajero

florist

florista

hairdresser

peluquero

conductor

cobrador

mechanic

mecánico

captain

capitán

dentist

dentista

scientist

científico

rabbi

rabino

imam

imán

monk

monje

clergyman

sacerdote

occupations - ocupaciones

tools
herramientas

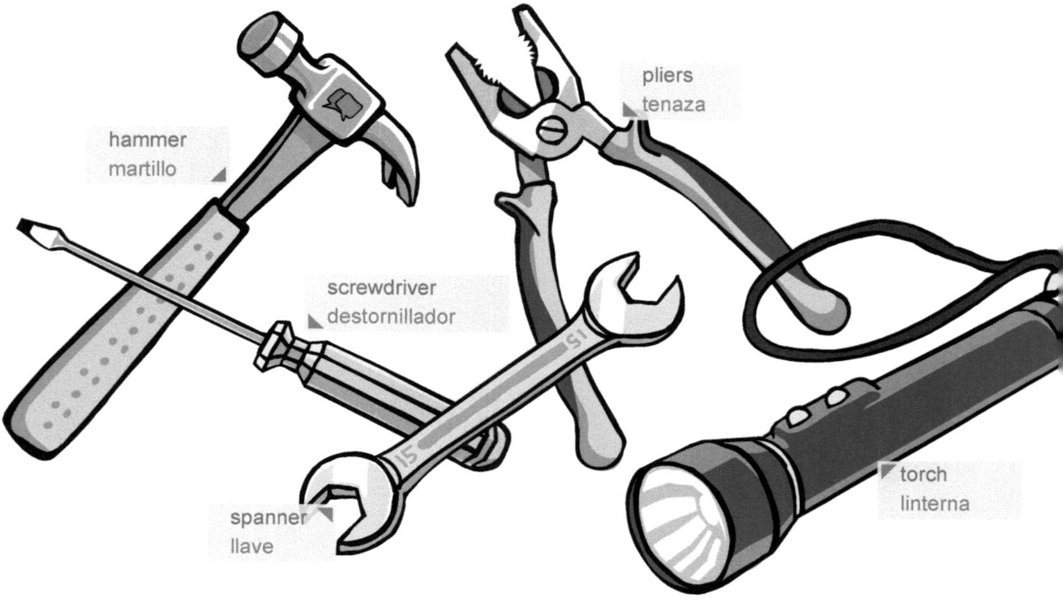

hammer
martillo
pliers
tenaza
screwdriver
destornillador
spanner
llave
torch
linterna

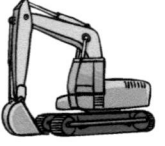

digger

excavadora

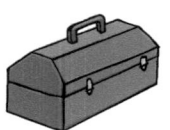

toolbox

caja de herramientas

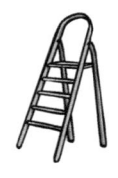

ladder

escalera portátil

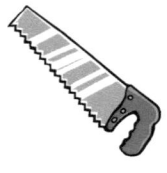

saw

sierra

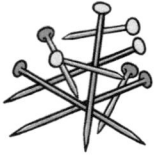

nails

clavos

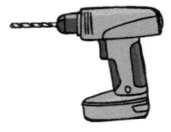

drill

taladro

repair

arreglar

shovel

pala de jardín

Damn!

¡Qué bronca!

dustpan

pala de plástico

paint pot

tacho de pintura

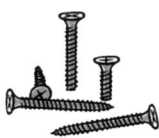

screws

tornillos

musical instruments
instrumentos musicales

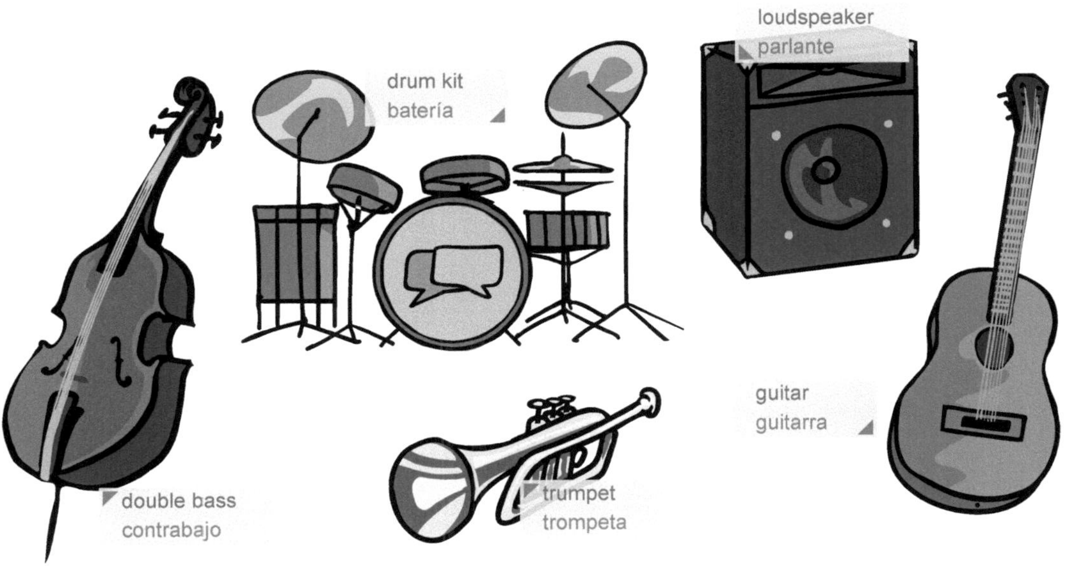

drum kit
batería

loudspeaker
parlante

guitar
guitarra

double bass
contrabajo

trumpet
trompeta

piano

piano

violin

violín

bass

bajo

timpani

timbales

drums

tambor

keyboard

teclado

saxophone

saxofón

flute

flauta

microphone

micrófono

entrance
entrada

tiger
tigre

cage
jaula

zebra
cebra

animal feed
alimento para animales

panda
oso panda

animals
animales

elephant
elefante

kangaroo
canguro

rhino
rinoceronte

gorilla
gorila

bear
oso

camel

camello

ostrich

avestruz

lion

león

monkey

mono

flamingo

flamenco

parrot

loro

polar bear

oso polar

penguin

pingüino

shark

tiburón

peacock

pavo real

snake

serpiente

crocodile

cocodrilo

zookeeper

cuidador del zoológico

seal

foca

jaguar

jaguar

zoo - zoológico

pony

poni

leopard

leopardo

hippo

hipopótamo

giraffe

jirafa

eagle

águila

boar

jabalí

fish

pescado

turtle

tortuga

walrus

morsa

fox

zorro

gazelle

gacela

zoo - zoológico

American football
fútbol americano

cycling
ciclismo

tennis
tenis

basketball
básquet

swimming
natación

boxing
boxeo

ice hockey
hockey sobre hielo

football
fútbol

badminton
bádminton

athletics
atletismo

handball
handball

skiing
esquí

polo
polo

laugh
reír

jump
saltar

hug
abrazar

walk
caminar

sing
cantar

dream
soñar

pray
rezar

kiss
besar

write
escribir

draw
dibujar

show
mostrar

push
presionar

give
dar

take
tomar

have

tener

do

hacer

be

ser

stand

estar parado

run

correr

pull

tirar

throw

tirar

fall

caer

lie

estar acostado

wait

esperar

carry

llevar

sit

estar sentado

get dressed

vestirse

sleep

dormir

wake up

despertar

look at

mirar

cry

llorar

stroke

acariciar

comb

peinar

talk

hablar

understand

entender

ask

preguntar

listen

escuchar

drink

beber

eat

comer

tidy up

ordenar

love

amar

cook

cocinar

drive

manejar

fly

volar

activities - actividades

sail

navegar

calculate

calcular

read

leer

learn

aprender

work

trabajar

marry

casarse

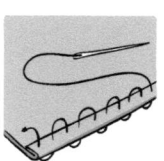

sew

coser

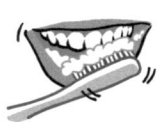

brush teeth

cepillarse los dientes

kill

matar

smoke

fumar

send

enviar

grandmother
abuela

grandfather
abuelo

father
padre

mother
madre

baby
bebé

daughter
hija

son
hijo

guest

invitado

aunt

tía

uncle

tío

brother

hermano

sister

hermana

body

cuerpo

forehead
frente
eye
ojo
shoulder
hombro
finger
dedo
face
cara
chin
pera
hand
mano
leg
pierna
breast
pecho
arm
brazo

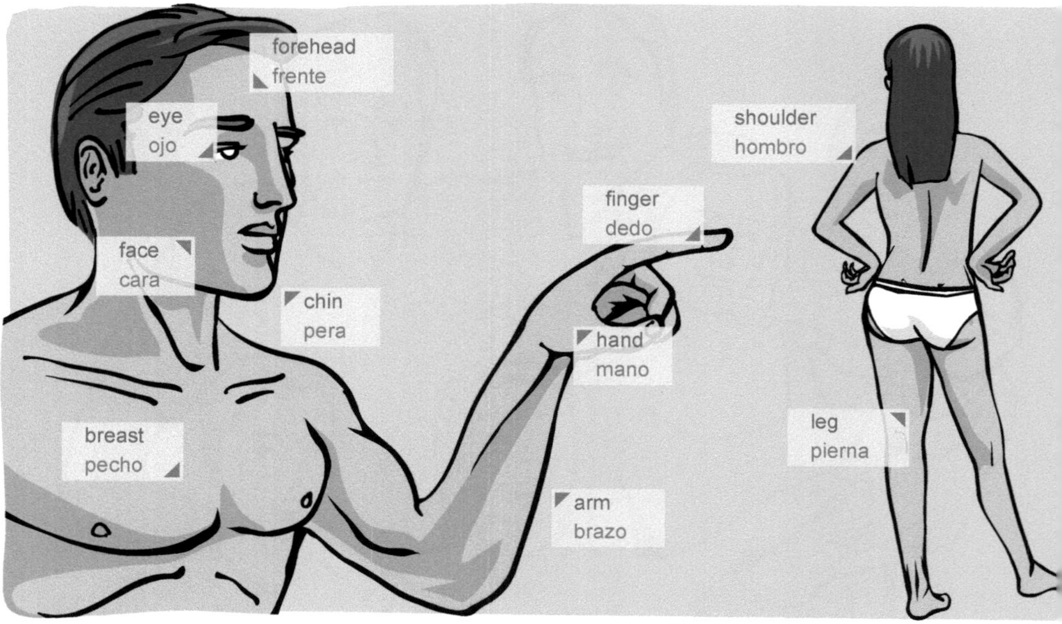

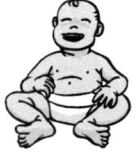

baby

bebé

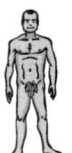

man

hombre

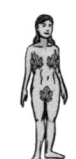

woman

mujer

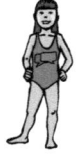

girl

nena

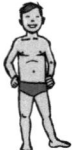

boy

nene

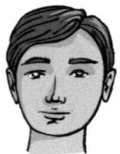

head

cabeza

back

espalda

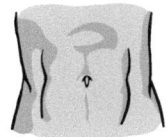

belly

panza

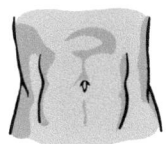

belly button

ombligo

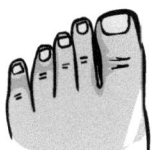

toe

dedo del pie

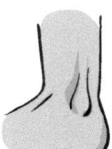

heel

talón

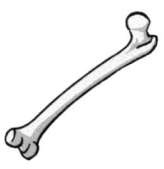

bone

hueso

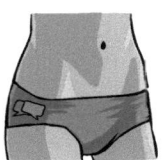

hip

cadera

knee

rodilla

elbow

codo

nose

nariz

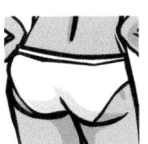

bottom

cola

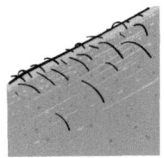

skin

piel

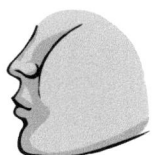

cheek

cachete

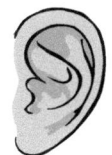

ear

oreja

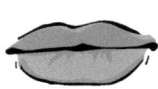

lip

labio

mouth

boca

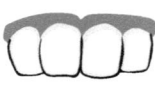

tooth

diente

tongue

lengua

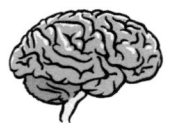

brain

cerebro

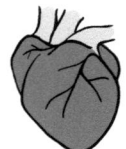

heart

corazón

muscle

músculo

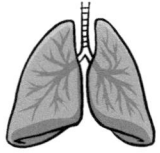

lung

pulmón

liver

hígado

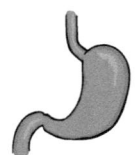

stomach

estómago

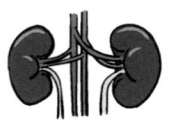

kidneys

riñones

sex

sexo

condom

preservativo

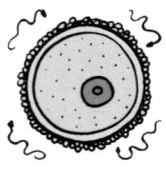

ovum

óvulo

semen

semen

pregnancy

embarazo

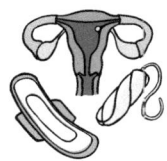

menstruation

menstruación

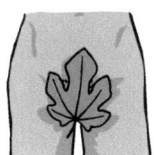

vagina

vagina

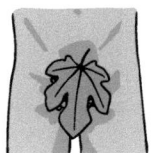

penis

pene

eyebrow

ceja

hair

pelo

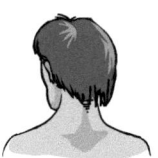

neck

cuello

hospital
hospital

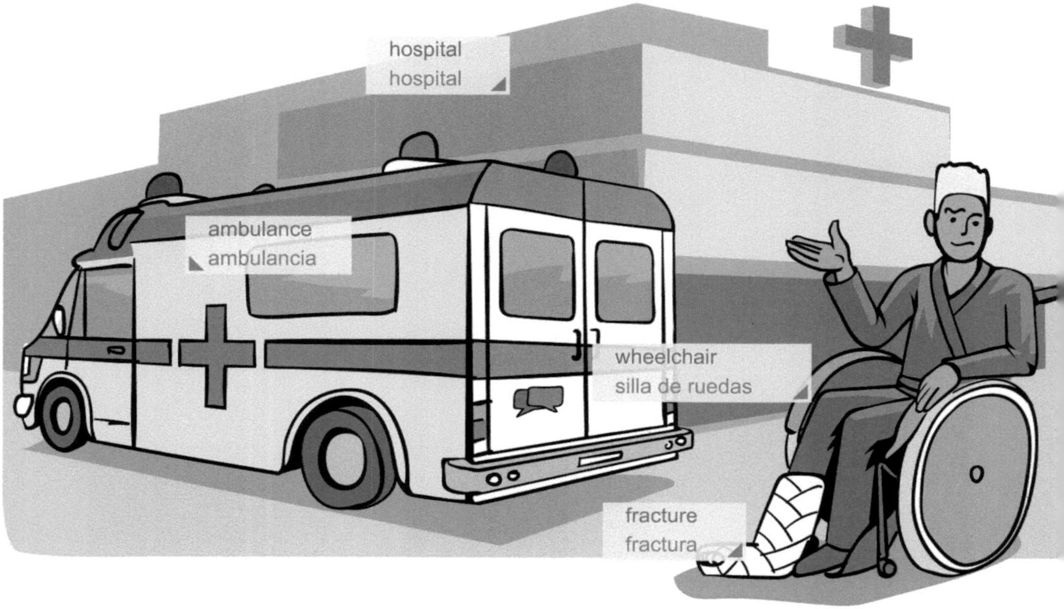

hospital
hospital
ambulance
ambulancia
wheelchair
silla de ruedas
fracture
fractura

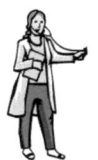

doctor
médico

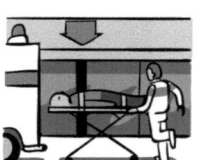

emergency room
sala de guardia

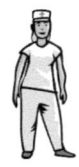

nurse
enfermera

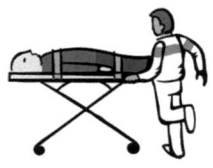

emergency
emergencia

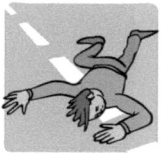

unconscious
inconsciente

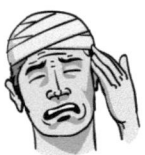

pain
dolor

injury

lesión

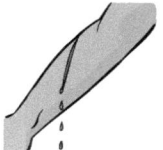

bleeding

hemorragia

heart attack

infarto

stroke

ACV

allergy

alergia

cough

tos

fever

fiebre

flu

gripe

diarrhoea

diarrea

headache

dolor de cabeza

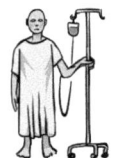

cancer

cáncer

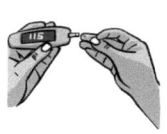

diabetes

diabetes

surgeon

cirujano

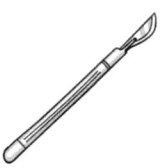

scalpel

bisturí

operation

operación

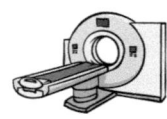

CT

TC

x-ray

rayos x

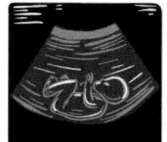

ultrasound

ecografía

face mask

barbijo

disease

enfermedad

waiting room

sala de espera

crutch

muleta

plaster

curita

bandage

venda

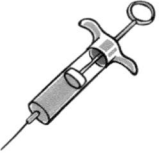

injection

inyección

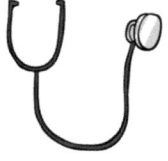

stethoscope

estetoscopio

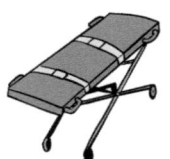

stretcher

camilla

clinical thermometer

termómetro

birth

nacimiento

overweight

sobrepeso

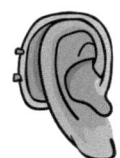

hearing aid

audífono

disinfectant

desinfectante

infection

infección

virus

virus

HIV / AIDS

VIH / SIDA

medicine

remedio

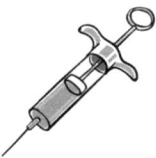

vaccination

vacunación

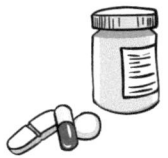

tablets

comprimidos

pill

pastilla anticonceptiva

emergency call

llamada de emergencia

blood pressure monitor

tensiómetro

ill / healthy

enfermo / sano

Help!
¡Ayuda!

alarm
alarma

assault
agresión

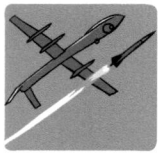

attack
ataque

danger
peligro

emergency exit
salida de emergencia

Fire!
¡Fuego!

fire extinguisher
matafuego

accident
accidente

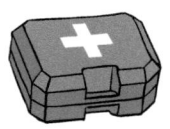

first-aid kit
botiquín de primeros auxilios

SOS
SOS

police
policía

Europe

Europa

North America

América del Norte

South America

América del Sur

Africa

África

Asia

Asia

Australia

Australia

Atlantic

Atlántico

Pacific

Pacífico

Indian Ocean

Océano Índico

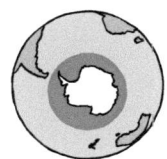

Antarctic Ocean

Océano Antártico

Arctic Ocean

Océano Ártico

North Pole

polo norte

South Pole
polo sur

Antarctica
Antártida

Earth
Tierra

land
tierra

sea
mar

island
isla

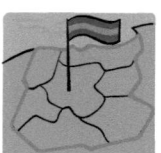

nation
nación

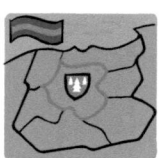

state
estado

clock face

esfera

hour hand

manecilla de las horas

minute hand

minutero

second hand

segundero

What time is it?

¿Qué hora es?

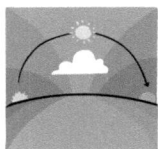

day

día

time

hora

now

ahora

digital watch

reloj digital

minute

minuto

hour

hora

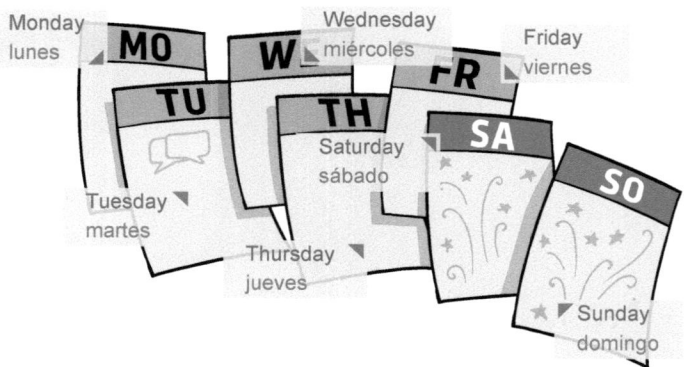

Monday / lunes
Wednesday / miércoles
Friday / viernes
Tuesday / martes
Saturday / sábado
Thursday / jueves
Sunday / domingo

yesterday

ayer

today

hoy

tomorrow

mañana

morning

mañana

noon

mediodía

evening

tarde

business days

días hábiles

weekend

fin de semana

year

año

rain
lluvia
wind
viento
snow
nieve
spring
primavera
summer
verano
autumn
otoño
winter
invierno

4.APRIL 11°
5.APRIL 4°
6.APRIL 13°
7.APRIL 8°
8.APRIL 10°

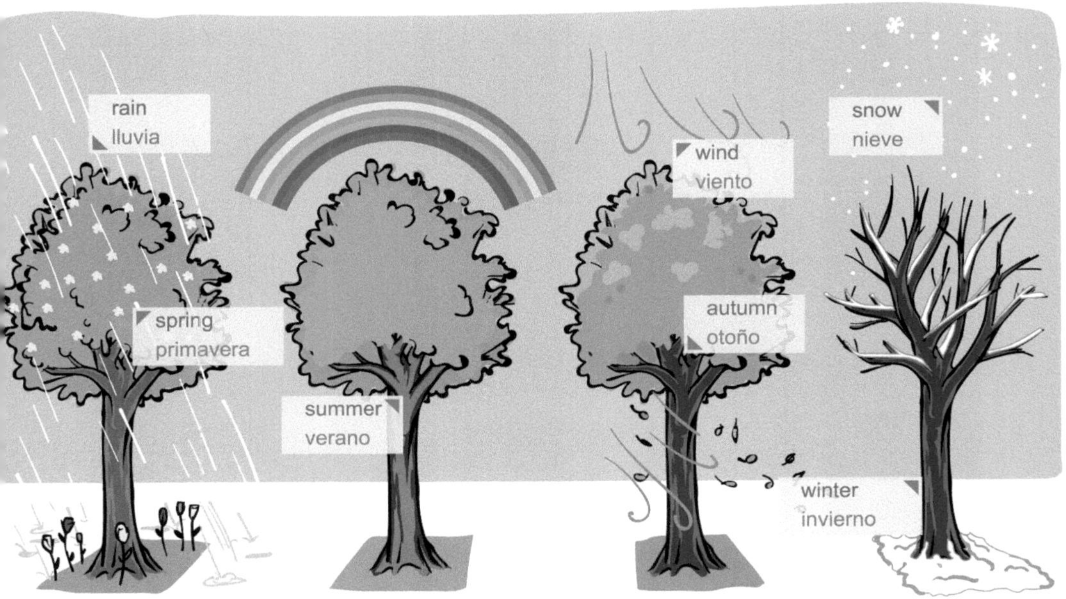

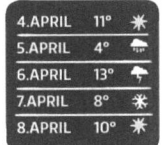

weather forecast

pronóstico meteorológico

F C
120 40
90 30
60 20
30 10
0 0
-30 -10
-20

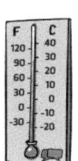

thermometer

termómetro

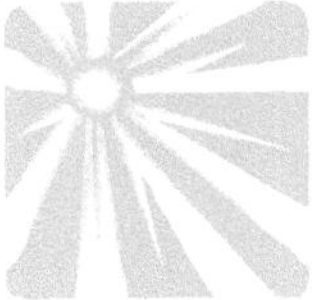

sunshine

luz del sol

cloud

nube

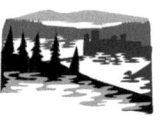

fog

niebla

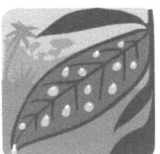

humidity

humedad

lightning

rayo

thunder

trueno

storm

tormenta

hail

granizo

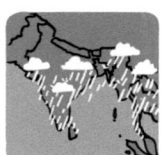

monsoon

monzón

flood

inundación

ice

hielo

January

enero

February

febrero

March

marzo

April

abril

May

mayo

June

junio

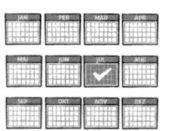

July

julio

August

agosto

September
....
septiembre

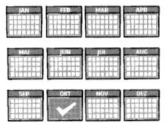

October
....
octubre

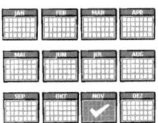

November
....
noviembre

December
....
diciembre

circle
....
círculo

square
....
cuadrado

rectangle
....
rectángulo

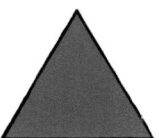

triangle
....
triángulo

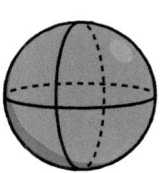

sphere
....
esfera

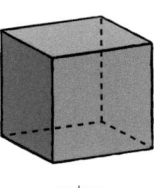

cube
....
cubo

colours
colores

white
blanco

yellow
amarillo

orange
naranja

pink
rosa

red
rojo

purple
violeta

blue
azul

green
verde

brown
marrón

grey
gris

black
negro

opposites
opuestos

a lot / a little
mucho / poco

angry / calm
enojado / tranquilo

beautiful / ugly
lindo / feo

beginning / end
principio / fin

big / small
grande / chico

bright / dark
claro / oscuro

brother / sister
hermano / hermana

clean / dirty
limpio / sucio

complete / incomplete
completo / incompleto

day / night
día / noche

dead / alive
muerto / vivo

wide / narrow
ancho / angosto

edible / inedible

comestible / no comestible

evil / kind

malo / amable

excited / bored

entusiasmado / aburrido

fat / thin

gordo / flaco

first / last

primero / último

friend / enemy

amigo / enemigo

full / empty

lleno / vacío

hard / soft

duro / blando

heavy / light

pesado / liviano

hunger / thirst

hambre / sed

ill / healthy

enfermo / sano

illegal / legal

ilegal / legal

intelligent / stupid

inteligente / estúpido

left / right

izquierda / derecha

near / far

cerca / lejos

new / used
nuevo / usado

nothing / something
nada / algo

old / young
viejo / joven

on / off
encendido / apagado

open / closed
abierto / cerrado

quiet / loud
silencioso / ruidoso

rich / poor
rico / pobre

right / wrong
correcto / incorrecto

rough / smooth
áspero / suave

sad / happy
triste / contento

short / long
corto / largo

slow / fast
lento / rápido

wet / dry
mojado / seco

warm / cool
caliente / frío

war / peace
guerra / paz

0

zero

cero

1

one

uno

2

two

dos

3

three

tres

4

four

cuatro

5

five

cinco

6

six

seis

7

seven

siete

8

eight

ocho

9

nine

nueve

10

ten

diez

11

eleven

once

12

twelve
doce

13

thirteen
trece

14

fourteen
catorce

15

fifteen
quince

16

sixteen
dieciséis

17

seventeen
diecisiete

18

eighteen
dieciocho

19

nineteen
diecinueve

20

twenty
veinte

100

hundred
cien

1.000

thousand
mil

1.000.000

million
millón

numbers - números

languages
idiomas

English
....
inglés

American English
....
inglés americano

Chinese Mandarin
....
chino mandarín

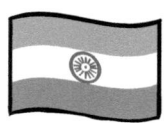

Hindi
....
hindi

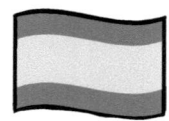

Spanish
....
español

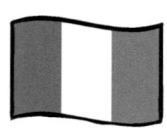

French
....
francés

Arabic
....
árabe

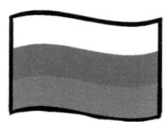

Russian
....
ruso

Portuguese
....
portugués

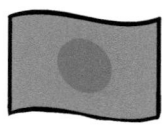

Bengali
....
bengalí

German
....
alemán

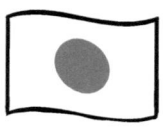

Japanese
....
japonés

I

yo

you

vos

he / she / it

él / ella

we

nosotros

you

ustedes

they

ellos

who?

¿quién?

what?

¿qué?

how?

¿cómo?

where?

¿dónde?

when?

¿cuándo?

name

nombre

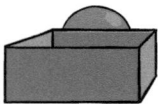

behind

detrás

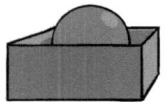

in

en

in front of

adelante de

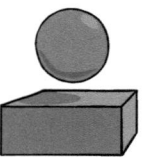

over

por encima de

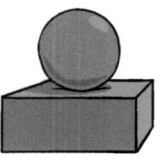

on

sobre

under

debajo de

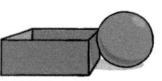

beside

al lado de

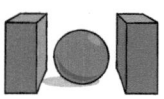

between

entre

place

lugar